WH.

I was introduced to Jim Harman in the late 1990s by his book *The Coming Spiritual Earthquake*. His new books on the Salvation of the Soul are dear to my heart, as it is so hard to see this teaching being dismissed within the body of Christ. I am thankful for his writings, and I completely agree with his findings that many believers will be extremely dismayed when the Lord returns, and they find themselves unprepared to meet Him.

       Robin Wade
       Manchester, NH

Reading *5 Warnings to Believers From the Book of Hebrews* strengthened my walk with the Lord in a very real way. James Harman brings out the seriousness of the five warnings in Hebrews and reminds us of the call to faithfulness that so many churches overlook today. Most Christians never hear teaching about the Kingdom, but Mr Harman presents these neglected biblical truths clearly. If you are serious about inheriting the Kingdom and living in a way that pleases the Lord, get this book. It challenged me, encouraged me, and sharpened my focus on what truly matters.

       Glenn Coyne
       Forest City, NC

Thank you so much for being obedient to God and writing your book: *5 Warnings to Believers – From the Book of Hebrews.* I so enjoy reading your books because they are easy to read and easy to understand. It is so wonderful to know that you are warning people. He will be coming back very soon to take His children home to our Heavenly Home. People need to repent of their sins and get ready to go. "Even so, come, Lord Jesus." (Revelation 22:20)

Ima Dean Jones
West Fork, AR

I enjoyed Jim Harman's *5 Warnings to Believers*. In his dedication, I appreciated that he correctly notes that Cindy and Jennifer have already entered New Jerusalem as a foretaste of their heavenly reward. I argued in my book, MMP5 that Heb 12:23 proves that faithful believers do indeed enter the Reward City, even before their public vindication at the Bema. He rightly confirms unfaithful believers will forfeit the possibility of reigning with Jesus in New Jerusalem, making the salvation of our souls a matter of eternal significance in relation to heavenly rewards.

Marty Cauley
Sylva, NC
www.misthology.org

5 WARNINGS

TO

BELIEVERS

From the Book of Hebrews

James T. Harman

**Prophecy
Countdown
Publications**

5 WARNINGS TO BELIEVERS

Copyright © 2026, James T. Harman
Prophecy Countdown Publications, LLC
P.O. Box 941612
Maitland, FL 32794
www.ProphecyCountdown.com

ISBN: 979-8-9928888-1-2 (Paperback)
ISBN: 979-8-9928888-2-9 (eBook)
ISBN: 979-8-9928888-3-6 (Audio)

All Rights Reserved. We encourage the use of this material; however, to protect the contents from changes, neither this book nor any part may be reprinted in any form without written permission from the publisher, except for brief excerpts used in reviews whereby the reviewer may quote brief passages with proper credit, and except for religious and educational purposes.

Scripture abbreviations are from the Blue Letter Bible (page 52).

Scripture is from the King James Version (KJV) unless noted.

Scripture quotations from the Amplified Bible (AMP) Copyright ©
  1987, by The Lockman Foundation. Used by permission.

Scripture quotations from the Thomson Chain Reference Bible,
  New International Version (NIV), Copyright 1973, 1978, and
  1984 by International Bible Society.

Scripture quotations from the New King James Version (NKJV)
  Copyright © 2013, by Holman Bible Publishers. All rights
  reserved.

Certain words, such as **Kingdom** and **Salvation of the Soul,** are
  capitalized to emphasize their importance, but not in accordance
  with Traditional fashion.

Numerical references to selected words in the text of Scripture are
  from James H. Strong's Dictionaries of the Hebrew-Greek words.

The Young's Literal Translation (YLT) was by Robert Young, who
  believed in a strictly literal translation of God's Word, and this
  version is in the public domain.

Credit for picture inside this book: Page 18 – Mount of Beatitudes.
  From prints taken between 1890 & 1900 in Capernaum, Israel.
  Similar prints may be viewed at: www.loc.gov

Back cover image depicting the Bride receiving a crown from
  Jesus by Kume Bryant, www.kumebryant.com

Dedication

This booklet is tenderly dedicated
To my wonderful wife, Cindy
And our beautiful daughter, Jennifer
Who recently went to their new Heavenly Homes
In the New Jerusalem.
(See Chapter 5 for more on how to get there).

To learn more about Cindy's incredible life
As well as her writings and memorial,
Please visit the Homepage of our website:
www.ProphecyCountdown.com

*There is laid up for me the **crown of righteousness**,*
which the Lord, the righteous Judge,
will give to me on that Day,
and not to me only but also
***to all who have loved His appearing**.*
(2Ti 4:8)

Looking for that blessed hope,
and the glorious appearing
of the great God and
our Saviour Jesus Christ.
(Titus 2:13 – KJV)

Books by the Author

Salvation of the Soul
  Continued cooperation with God's sanctification
Esdra's Three-Headed Eagle
  Three final rulers of the Earth
The Final Countdown
  Second Fulfilment of Daniel's Decree
The Open Door
  Vital preparation for the coming Kingdom
Daniel's Prophecies Unsealed
  Top-10 Bestseller of Daniel's 5 Visions
Come Away My Beloved
  Preparation for the Bride from Song of Solomon
Calling All Overcomers
  Preparation guide from the book of Revelation
Overcomers' Guide to the Kingdom
  Christ's teachings from the Sermon on the Mount
The Glorious Gospel
  God's final plan for mankind
The Kingdom
  God's reward for the salvation of the soul
Don't Be Left Behind
  A look at God's timing during the last days
The Coming Spiritual Earthquake
  The coming separation at the Rapture
Beyond the Higher Power
  Steps to overcome addiction to drugs & alcohol
The Blessed Hope
  Looking for the Glorious Appearing of our Lord

Prologue

This booklet addresses the five warnings found in the book of Hebrews. There is much controversy surrounding who these warnings are meant for. This brief study will show why these warnings are for individuals who have come to believe on the Lord Jesus Christ as their own personal Saviour.

Once God's marvellous grace saves us, we receive the free gift of eternal life (Eph 2:8-9). This past aspect, known as justification by faith, is a work of God in our lives. After we become justified by faith, believers have a choice to make. Those who decide to be followers of Christ become His disciples. On the other hand, many believers decide that being a disciple of Christ will require more than they are prepared for (see Luk 9:23-25).

As I began writing this booklet, the Lord graciously reminded me that I need to listen to the message in this work as much as the audience for whom I am writing it!

The five warnings in the book of Hebrews have an enormous bearing on where and how believers will experience their future in the coming age. This truth is also corroborated by Arlen Chitwood's insightful observations:

> "The five major warnings in the Book of Hebrews and the seven overcomers' promises in the Book of Revelation, in this respect, have to do with *the SAME thing*. They are *BOTH* Messianic in their outlook and are directed to the saved, not the unsaved. And *BOTH* have to do, *NOT* with the salvation which we presently possess, *BUT* with the **salvation of the soul**.
>
> It is the *overcomer* (Rev. 2, 3) who will realize *"so great salvation"* (Heb. 2:3) and be allowed to ascend the throne as a *companion* with God's Son during the coming age (*cf.* Heb 1:8,9,14; 3:14 Rev 3:21).
>
> And in the Book of Hebrews [1:5-13], the picture is that of Christ as *King*, with the *overcomers* from the Churches seated with Him on the throne [a scene presenting *Christ and His co-heirs*...holding the sceptre together during the Messianic Era...]"[1]

The question for the reader is very simple. Will you decide to be a disciple of Jesus Christ? If so, you will be so very glad that you did!

---

1) Arlen L. Chitwood, ***So Great Salvation,*** (The Lamp Broadcast, Cottonwood, AZ 2020): 8-9

Table of Contents

Prologue vii

Foreword xi

Introduction 13

Warning # 1 Don't Neglect Great Salvation 17
  Hebrews 2:1-5
Warning # 2 Don't Harden Your Heart 23
  Hebrews 3:12-15 to 4:13
Warning # 3 Don't Turn Back to the World 29
  Hebrews 6:4-8
Warning # 4 Don't Cast Away Your Confidence 35
  Hebrews 10:26-39
Warning # 5 Don't Refuse to Listen to Him 43
  Hebrews 12:22-29
Epilogue 49

Bibliography 51
Appendix – Signs of Christ's Coming 53
Special Invitation 61
Looking For the Son 73

3) The voice of one crying in the wilderness:

*"**Prepare the way of the Lord**;*
Make straight in the desert
A highway for our God.
*4) **Every valley shall be exalted***
And every mountain and hill brought low;
The crooked places shall be made straight
And the rough places smooth;
*5) **The glory of the Lord shall be revealed**,*
And all flesh shall see it together;
For the mouth of the Lord has spoken."
(Isaiah 40:3-5 – NKJV)

John the Baptist Prepares the Way
In those days John the Baptist came preaching
in the wilderness of Judea, and saying,
"Repent for the
Kingdom of heaven is at hand!"

For this is he who was spoken of
by the prophet Isaiah…
(Matthew 3:1-3 – NKJV)

Foreword

I am amazed at the extent to which preachers, Bible teachers, and commentators interpret Scripture through the lens of systematic theology, rather than relying on proper historical and grammatical exegesis of the biblical text. This hermeneutical error has been perpetuated for centuries, dating back to the Reformation.

One of the results of this dreadful mistake is misinterpreting the Letter to the Hebrews as a warning to those who merely *think* they are believers, whereas their behavior demonstrates they are not. The epistle, in that case, is seen as a call to salvation or, at the very least, a plea to persevere in good behavior in order to attain final salvation at the judgment. This common interpretation is theologically driven, for Scripture, rightfully interpreted, does not teach that one's salvation in Jesus Christ is confirmed or maintained by behavior; otherwise, Scripture would be teaching works-based salvation.

James Harman takes the correct position that the epistle to the Hebrews was written to believers, to encourage us to persevere in discipleship all the way to the Judgment Seat of Christ, so we can be rewarded. The five warnings in Hebrews, therefore, are intended as "wake-up calls" to urge believers to prepare for the account we will give to Jesus as to how we live the Christian life in this present age.

Christ's verdict will determine our inheritance for the next age—the kingdom age—when Jesus rules over Earth for a thousand years. Unfaithful believers will not be rewarded and will be relegated to the darkness outside (*cf.* the parable of the talents, Matt. 25:14-30). Good and faithful believers, on the other hand, will be given the glorious reward of inheriting New Jerusalem, the privilege of dwelling with Jesus in the ruling realm of the millennial kingdom, where they will serve as His bride and co-regents.

If you are a child of God, I would urge you to take this booklet seriously, for it seeks to interpret Hebrews correctly and challenges us to prepare to meet the Lord. The attitude that believers are automatically prepared by the nature of the fact that they have been saved is pharisaical.

In Matt. 3, when the Pharisees heard John the Baptist urging them to repent, they replied, *"We have Abraham as our father."* That arrogant reply is essentially the thinking that believers are already prepared because they are believers, and therefore, in good standing with God. Remarkably, that same erroneous way of thinking is widely accepted today in evangelical Christianity. Undoubtedly, there will be great shock and surprise at the Judgment Seat of Christ.

This excellent booklet can be used as an expanded tract, of sorts, *for believers*, to help us understand the urgency of getting our lives in order, in cooperation with God. There is much at stake!

> James S. Hollandsworth
> Pastor and Author
> TruthOverTraditions.com

Introduction

The book of Hebrews is one of the books in our Bibles that has been greatly debated and misunderstood by many believers. Who wrote the book is also highly disputed, with some suggesting Apollos or Barnabas as the author. The controversy is easily solved when we listen to the explanation given by Harry A. Ironside, a prolific author who pastored Moody Church in Chicago from 1929 to 1948:

> "In Peter's second letter, he identifies for us the author, under God, of the Epistle to the Hebrews. He mentions a letter written to Jewish believers by our beloved brother Paul, *'in which are some things hard to be understood'* ...As we know, Peter's special ministry was to the circumcision, and he addressed his letters to Christian Jews of the Diaspora, that is, those dispersed among the Gentiles. The letter to the Hebrews, therefore, must be that referred to in the verses quoted, as no other of Paul's Epistles is addressed to the Hebrew believers. And surely there is no other letter in the New Testament which contains more difficult statements than this one."[2]

---

2) Harry A. Ironside, Litt.D., *Except Ye Repent* (Baker Book House, Grand Rapids, MI, 1937): 127

Robert Govett also believes the Apostle Paul wrote this Epistle to the Hebrews, noting:

> "Paul as the first to proclaim Jesus as "the Son of God" (Acts ix. 20); and that is the key-note of this Epistle...The believers to whom the Epistle is addressed were suffering persecution...Some had fallen back to Judaism...Especially, they had lost firm hold of the **Saviour's coming** and **Kingdom**, and this **letter was designed to re-awaken their faith and hope in that great truth**."[3] (emphasis added)

The Apostle Paul recognized that the gospel message was in danger of falling back to the law. He tells them that God has appointed His Son to be heir over all things, having purged our sins, and is awaiting that wonderful day when He will come into possession of His inheritance:

> *1) God, who at various times and in various ways spoke to the fathers by the prophets, 2) has **in these last days** spoken to us by **His Son**, whom He has **appointed heir** of all things, through whom also He made the worlds...3) and upholding all things by **the word of His power**; when He had by Himself **purged our sins**, sat down at the right hand of the Majesty on high, 4) having become so much better than the angels, as He has **by inheritance** obtained a **more excellent** name than they.* (Hbr1:1-4 – NKJV)

---

3) Robert Govett, ***Govett On Hebrews*** (Schoettle Publishing, Hayesville, NC, 2010): 3

INTRODUCTION

The Son then becomes the central focus of the book of Hebrews. After showing how much greater the Son is than the angels, he gives seven messianic quotations from the Old Testament that point us toward the coming Kingdom of our Lord (Psa 2:7, 2 Sam 7:14, Deu 32:43, Psa 97:7, Psa 104:4, Psa 45:6, 7, Psa 102:25-27, Psa 110:1).

Notice that the angel's job has now changed: *"Are they not all ministering spirits sent forth to minister for **those who will inherit** salvation?"* (Hbr 1:14)

Now that the Son has ended His earthly mission and is exalted above the angels, their new role is to minister to those who will *inherit* salvation. Those who will inherit this salvation are all those individuals who will become disciples of the Son.

Govett reveals there are two aspects to this salvation: "...it should be observed that the word translated 'inherit' means to 'partake' – whether by inheritance, or gift, or effort. 'Salvation' has two aspects.

1) *Eternal life* - God's **present gift** to everyone that believes...
2) And *The First Resurrection*, or the ***millennial kingdom***, which is **to be sought for by the believer with all his might**. For it is the '**reward**' of service to Christ. This Epistle [Hebrews] speaks of salvation ***as yet future***;

for it looks onward to the completion of it in resurrection; hence its many exhortations to diligence."[4] (emphasis added)

The Book of Hebrews shows the two primary aspects of the believer's salvation. First, we are saved by God's marvelous gift:

*8) For by **grace** <u>you have been saved</u> through **faith**, and that not of yourselves; it is the <u>gift of God</u>, 9) <u>not of works</u>, lest anyone should boast.* (Eph 2:8-9)

After we become saved, God wants us to carry out the plans He intended for us in Ephesians 2:10:

10) For we are His workmanship, <u>created</u> in Christ Jesus <u>for good works</u>, which God prepared [ordained – KJV] beforehand that <u>we should walk in them</u>.

The salvation mentioned in Hebrews deals primarily with this second aspect of our salvation. It is known as the **salvation of the soul**, which represents the ongoing process of sanctification. It embodies a continuing work of God in our life that requires our cooperation: *"...<u>work out your own salvation</u> with fear and trembling; for it is God who works in you both to will and to do for His good pleasure"* (Phl 2:12-13).

The 5 warnings given in the Book of Hebrews are given to exhort believers to be faithful to God's calling for us.

---

4) Ibid., 28

Warning # 1

Don't Neglect Great Salvation

The second chapter of Hebrews introduces the focal point of God's message to believers.

*1) Therefore, we must give the more earnest heed to the things we have heard, lest we drift away. 2) For if the word spoken through angels proved steadfast, and **every** transgression and disobedience **received a just reward**, 3) how shall we escape if we **neglect [ignore – NIV] so great a salvation**, which at the **first began to be spoken by the Lord,** and was confirmed to us by those who heard Him,* (Hbr 2:1-3 – NKJV)

After telling us about how much greater the Son is than the angels, the Apostle Paul warns us not to ignore such a *great salvation* that is being offered to us.

So Great Salvation
The traditional understanding of which aspect of salvation is being discussed relates to our initial belief in Jesus Christ for eternal life, i.e., being "born again." While coming to Christ is one of the most wonderful events in our lives, this is not the aspect of salvation that Paul was addressing.

The salvation being addressed has to do with the aspect *"that first began to be spoken by the Lord."* At the very beginning of Christ's ministry, He gathered His disciples together on the top of the Mount of Beatitudes.

This mountain is located approximately a mile from the Sea of Galilee. Here, Jesus taught His disciples the new principles to help them prepare for the coming Kingdom. The Sermon on the Mount was delivered by our Lord to teach His disciples what their new life was to be like, including: *"...seek first the Kingdom of God and His righteousness, and all these things shall be added to you."* (Mat 6:33 – NKJV).

Then, near the very end of the Lord's ministry, He took the disciples to the region of Caesarea Philippi: *"Then said Jesus unto his disciples, If any man will come after me, let him deny himself and*

WARNING # 1 *Don't Neglect Great Salvation*

take up his cross, and follow me" (Mat 16:24).

These new instructions Jesus gave were entirely different. They were directed at those who want to be devoted pupils of His teachings. These new guidelines require works, i.e., 1) deny self, 2) take up his cross, and 3) follow me. These crucial instructions on the **salvation of the soul** are for believers who want to be His disciples. As noted by eminent lawyer Philip Mauro, "The salvation of the soul is distinctly referred to as something ***future***, and as something ***conditional upon the behavior of the individual himself.*** In the words of the Lord Himself, not as a gift, but as a reward to be earned by diligence, stead-fastness, and obedience to His commands."[5]

The **great salvation** that believers are told not to neglect or ignore is the ***salvation of the soul***, which Jesus first introduced to His disciples during His three and one-half years of ministry. The first warning in the book of Hebrews is for believers not to ignore or neglect Christ's teachings on the salvation of the soul. Unfortunately, the subject of the *salvation of the soul* is rarely taught today. Most believers only understand the first aspect of their salvation or the *salvation of the spirit*, which occurs when they are born again.

---

5) Philip Mauro, ***God's Pilgrims*** (Schoettle Publishing, Hayesville, NC, 2010): 136

The **great salvation** being addressed in the Book of Hebrews pertains to the future aspect, which **faithful** believers will realize when they stand before the Judgment Seat of Christ. This great salvation has to do with our heavenly inheritance in the coming Kingdom. Jesus told His disciples to *"seek first the **Kingdom of God** and His righteousness...."* (Mat 6:33). This is the main focus that the great salvation is concerned with.

And this is the aspect of our salvation that Apostle Paul is warning us not to neglect. The Greek word for neglect (G 272) is *ameleo*, which means to be unconcerned about or to care little about it. Most believers today pay very little attention to the coming Kingdom of God. Most of the church focuses on being saved, while completely ignoring our future salvation. This is precisely what Paul is warning us not to do. Let's see why the warnings.

Escape What?
The warning given in Hebrews 2:3 tells us not to ignore our great salvation, because to do so would result in receiving a just recompense of reward, i.e., we would **not** receive a reward due to our disobedience (neglect).

> *2) For if the word spoken through angels proved steadfast, and every transgression and **disobedience** <u>received a just reward,</u>*
> *3) **how shall we escape** if we **neglect [ignore –** NIV**] so great a salvation**,...* (Hbr 2:3 – NKJV)

Israel in the Wilderness

A perfect example of how disobedience received a just recompense of reward is found in the history of Israel. God saved Israel out of Egypt, and their future inheritance was to be the Promised Land of Canaan. However, because they disobeyed by not believing God, they were not allowed to enter. All except Caleb and Joshua were overthrown in the wilderness (*cf.* 1Co 10:1-12, Num 13 & 14).

Similarly, believers are on a pilgrimage journey with the heavenly aspect of our future salvation in view, i.e., the Kingdom of God. D.M. Panton tells us: "So the Rest is the Millennial Reign. For it is the sabbath rest, or seventh millennium, following on six thousand years of redemption toil…Thus, Canaan is the type of the Millennial Kingdom of Christ."[6]

The warning given in Hebrews is not to neglect this teaching on the Great Salvation. Unfortunately, most believers pay little attention to the salvation of the soul and the reward of our future inheritance in the coming Kingdom of God.

The great danger for many believers is that their lack of interest could cause them to miss the glorious opportunity of ruling and reigning with Jesus Christ in the coming Kingdom of God.

---

6) D.M. Panton, ***The Judgment Seat of Christ***
(Schoettle Publishing, Hayesville, NC, 1984): 40

SEEK FIRST THE KINGDOM

If you have read this far in this booklet, perhaps the Holy Spirit has led you here. If you are a believer, do you go to church? Many people receive Christ as their personal Saviour and don't attend a fellowship with other believers. I would strongly encourage you to seek out a local congregation where they teach the Word of God and become a disciple of our Lord (Hbr 10:24-25, Phl 2:12-13).

Perhaps you are a believer, but you have never really considered the teachings in the Book of Hebrews. If you have read this far, I would encourage you to continue reading the final four warnings.

God has a marvelous future in store for all those believers who want to know Him better. One of the purposes of this writing is to ignite a flame in your heart to draw closer to Him by studying His Word.

> "...*seek first the Kingdom of God*
> *and His righteousness, and*
> *all these things shall be added to you.*"
> (Mat 6:33 – NKJV)

Those faithful believers who are earnestly seeking the Kingdom of God and not neglecting this Great Salvation will be magnificently rewarded with their glorious inheritance in the coming Kingdom.

Warning # 2

Don't Harden Your Heart

The third and fourth chapters of Hebrews continue with exhortations for believers to be faithful, using examples from the Old Testament:

> *7) Therefore, as the Holy Spirit says: 'Today, if you will hear His voice, 8) **Do not harden your hearts** as in the rebellion, In the day of trial in the wilderness, 9) Where your fathers tested Me, tried Me, And saw My works forty years, 10) Therefore I was angry with that generation, And said, 'They always go astray in their heart, And they have not known My ways.' 11) So I swore in My wrath, **They shall not enter My rest**.*
> (Hbr 3:7-11 – NKJV)

After reminding these believers not to ignore the great salvation that is being offered to them in the previous chapter, the Apostle Paul gives them an example, quoting from Psalm 95:7-11.

Moses had led them out of Egypt for the purpose of bringing them into the Promised Land of Canaan. Remember, Canaan serves as a type for the Millennial Kingdom of Christ. Paul is exhorting them not to follow in the same footsteps as the Israelite people did, lest they might fall short of the goal of their faith.

12) Beware, brethren, lest there be any of you an evil [sinful – NIV] heart of unbelief in departing from the living God; 13) but exhort one another daily, while it is called "Today," lest any of you be hardened through the deceitfulness of sin. (Hbr 3:12-13 – NKJV)

This is a stern admonition to believers not to turn away from the Lord in their Christian pilgrimage. Remember, sin can be deceitful by tricking us into drifting away from righteousness. It may seem appealing or harmless, but it could lead to a stubborn, unrepentant attitude toward God.

The great danger from *"a heart of unbelief in departing from the living God"* is that it could result in being disinherited from entering into God's rest, which would mean not ruling and reigning with Christ in His Millennial Kingdom. Don't follow the example of Israel. They wandered in the wilderness for 40 years, and all except Caleb and Joshua died in the wilderness (*cf.* 1Co 10:1-12, Num 13 & 14).

Paul is warning us not to allow this to happen, but to exhort one another every day. Don't stop walking with Jesus. Allow Him to empower and direct your life every day!

*14) For we [believers] have become partakers of Christ [sharing in all that the Messiah has for us], **if only** we hold firm our newborn confidence*

[which originally led us to Him] until the end, 15) while it is said,
"TODAY [while there is still opportunity]
IF YOU HEAR HIS VOICE, DO NOT HARDEN YOUR HEART, AS WHEN THEY PROVOKED ME [in the rebellion in the desert at Meribah]."
(Hbr 3:14-15 – AMP)

Sharing Heavenly Hope

If you are a believer, you can become a partaker or a companion of Jesus Christ. He wants to share an incredible future with you. The inheritance that He has planned for you is a heavenly hope beyond anything you can imagine. However, this verse introduces a condition to this hope. It says we need to have the same confidence as Caleb and Joshua because they believed God would help them take the land of Canaan. They were not like all the Israelites who rebelled and lost their inheritance.

Caleb and Joshua serve as types for those believers who will enter that future rest in the heavenly Kingdom if we do not harden our hearts and ignore God's promises of our future hope.

*11) Let us therefore **be diligent** to **enter that rest**, lest anyone fall according to the same example of disobedience. 12) For the **word of God** is living and powerful, and sharper than any two-edged sword...13) And there is no creature hidden from His sight, but all things are*

> *naked and open to the eyes of Him whom **we must give account***. (Hbr 4:11-13 – NKJV)

Judgment Seat of Christ

You can find the Apostle Paul's teachings on the coming day all believers will "give account" for their lives in 1 Corinthians 3:10-17 and 2 Corinthians 5:9-11. In Hebrews, he is admonishing us to be diligent to make sure we do not harden our hearts and fall short like Israel did.

Faithful believers who have persevered in their faith will hear the Lord tell them: *"Well done, good and faithful servant...Enter into the joy of your Lord"* (Mat 25:21). This will be one of their most joyful experiences in their life!

However, many believers will arrive before Jesus, with little to show for their lives. Like the Israelites who turned back to the wilderness, the unfaithful servants will not enter the Millennial Kingdom to rule and reign with the Lord.

As Martha Lever so beautifully illustrates for us:
> "The goal of our faith is the salvation of our souls. The salvation of the soul will be completed and manifested at the Judgment Seat of Christ when the Christian's works (gold, silver, precious stones, wood, hay, or stubble) will be tested by fire.

WARNING # 2 *Don't Harden Your Heart*

> If our works withstand the test of fire and we are left with gold, silver, and precious stones, then our souls will be saved, and we will receive our reward. The reward will be a position of rulership in the 1,000-year kingdom of Jesus Christ when He returns to rule the earth. Only the 'work' that the Holy Spirit accomplished ***through us*** will stand at the Judgment Seat of Christ. Those whose souls are not saved at the Judgment Seat of Christ will not receive their reward – a position in the millennial kingdom."[7]

Martha's illustration should be a sobering warning for many believers who have not been living their lives for Jesus nor actively in the process of saving their souls.

Remember, the salvation of the soul represents the ongoing process of sanctification. It embodies a continuing work of God in our lives that requires our cooperation as the Apostle Paul teaches us in Philippians 2:12-13: *"...**work out your own salvation** with fear and trembling; for it is God who works in you both to will and to do for His good pleasure."*

---

7) Martha Lever, ***Rightly Dividing The Word of Truth*** (Schoettle Publishing, Austin, TX, 2021): 10

Today, while there is still time, all believers need to examine their spiritual condition, making sure that Jesus is the center of their lives.

The salvation of the soul is rarely discussed in the Church today; however, as the first warning has shown, it is the ***great salvation*** we are admonished not to neglect or ignore.

For many of our readers, this may be the first time they have ever heard about this subject. We highly recommend that you consult many of the books in the Bibliography for further reading on this subject.

Also, we recommend our latest book: ***Salvation of the Soul***, which can be freely downloaded on our website: www.ProphecyCountdown.com.

Chapters 3 and 4 in that book provide a helpful analysis of how the book of James addresses this critical aspect of the believer's salvation.

1) Come, all you who are thirsty, come to the waters;
And you who have no money, come, buy and eat!
Come, buy wine and milk without money, without cost.
2) Why spend money on what is not bread?
And your labor on what does not satisfy?
Listen, listen to me, and eat what is good,
And you will delight in the richest of fare.
(Isaiah 55:1-2 – NIV)

Warning # 3

Don't Turn Back to the World

The third warning to believers is found in chapter 6 in the Book of Hebrews and is probably one of the most challenging passages that you can find in the entire Bible.

4) For it is impossible for those who were once enlightened, and have tasted the heavenly gift, and have become partakers of the Holy Spirit, and have tasted the good word of God and the powers of the age^{G165} to come, 6) if they fall away, to renew them again to repentance, since they crucify again for themselves the Son of God, and put Him to open shame.
(Hbr 6:4-6 – NKJV)

It is essential to understand that the above passage describes mature believers in Christ. It lists five characteristics that depict Christians who have been saved and become *partakers* (partners) with the Holy Spirit and understand the *"powers of age to come,"* where the Greek word *Aion* (G 165) is used, which portrays Christ's coming Millennial Kingdom.

These believers are Christians who have been saved and seen the power of God in their lives. God is warning them not to fall away from the secure path they are on, for it would be impossible to restore them if they were to turn away.

Many have misunderstood these verses to mean that the Christian would lose their salvation. This is not what this warning is for. Once a person becomes saved, i.e., they have been "born again" by believing in Jesus for their salvation, they can never lose that precious gift.

All of the warnings given in the Book of Hebrews relate to the believer's rewards and not their eternal salvation, which is completely secure.

Warning of Being a Castaway
Here in Hebrews, the Apostle Paul is warning us not to fall away. To do so, it would be impossible *to renew them again to repentance.* This stern warning is for believers: if you turn away, it will be impossible for you to receive any rewards.

In other words, when they stand before the Judgment Seat of Christ, they will not hear *"Well done, good and faithful servant..."* but rather they will lose their inheritance in the coming Millennial Kingdom. They will forever forfeit the opportunity to reign with Jesus in the New Jerusalem.

WARNING # 3 *Don't Turn Back to the World*

Similarly, the Apostle Paul also told the Corinthian believers using the metaphor of the prize:

> *24) Know ye not that they which run in a race run all, but one receiveth the **prize**? So run, that ye may obtain. 27) But I keep under my body, and bring it into subjection: lest that by any means, when I have preached to others, I myself should be a castaway.* (1 Cr 9:24, 27 – KJV)

The great Apostle Paul realized that we are all in a race that requires faithful perseverance to receive the prize. He realized that even he could become disqualified for the reward and become a castaway.

[When we get to the fifth warning in Hebrews, we will see that the prize Paul is referring to represents the City of Reward found in Hebrews 12:22-23.]

It is important to point out that this third warning is for believers to highlight the grave danger that exists if they stop following the Lord and turn back to living for themselves. Christians must persevere in their faith by living for the Lord every day. The believer who turns back to the world needs to realize that to do so would mean that "the repentance spoken in Hebrews 6:6 is on God's part, not the individual's part."[8]

---

8) Scott Crawford, *Five Warnings for Believers* (Schoettle Publishing, Hayesville, NC, 2006): 27

In other words, the third warning in Hebrews is an admonition to believers to stay the course, keep pressing on for the prize, don't give up! God will help you if you allow Him. The late M.R. DeHaan noted how the passage in Hebrews six is explained by the passage in Philippians 3:14: "I press toward the mark [finish line, the goal] for the prize [crown] of the high calling of God in Christ Jesus...He is speaking of Christians who began the race but fell by the wayside. There comes a time after repeated warnings and admonitions, the Christian continues in disobedience...until God shelves him, to deal with him at the Judgment Seat of Christ."[9]

Blessing or Curse
7) For the earth which drinks in the rain that often comes upon it, and bears herbs useful for those by whom it is cultivated, receives blessing from God, 8) but if it bears thorns and briers, it is rejected and near to being cursed, whose end is to be burned (Hbr 6:7-8 – NKJV).

Paul then uses the above metaphor to show the two different types of believers. The first one that produces useful crops is faithful and receives a reward from the Lord. The second one, however, is rejected due to their own neglectful life.

---

9) M.R. DeHaan, ***Studies in Hebrews*** (Kregel Publications, Grand Rapids, MI, 49501): 101

WARNING # 3 *Don't Turn Back to the World*

The believer whose life produces thorns and briers is about to be burned up. At this point, many Christians will object and say that this can't possibly describe a true believer!

However, their incorrect assessment has failed to consider the following teaching by Paul:

> *12) Now if anyone builds on this foundation with gold, silver, precious stones, wood, hay, straw, 13) each one's work will become clear; for the Day will declare it, because it will be revealed by fire; and the fire will test each one's work, of what sort it is. 14) If anyone's work, which he has built on it endures, he will receive a reward. 15) If anyone's **work is burned**, he will suffer loss; but **he himself will be saved**, yet **so as through fire*** (1 Cr 3:12-15 – NKJV).

Pastor James Hollandsworth provides a very valuable explanation: "After passing through the furnace of fire, some will come out unscathed (like the three Hebrew men in Babylon), for their works will be of the quality of gold, silver, and precious stones. The fire will not hurt them...But other Christians will lose everything...They will be saved, yet so as by (through) fire."[10]

---

10) James Hollandsworth, ***The End of the Pilgrimage*** (Holly Publishing, Lexington, KY):141

After giving these stern warnings, he encourages the believers by saying:

> *9) But beloved, we are confident of better things concerning you, yes, things that accompany salvation [Rewards]. 10) For God is not unjust to forget your work and labor of love which you have shown toward His name, in that you have ministered to the saints, and do minister.*
> (Hbr 6:9-10 – NKJV)

Therefore, former pastor M.R. DeHaan cautions us: "Christian, walk carefully, with your eye on the goal. How fitting the conclusion of this passage:
> *That ye be not slothful, but followers of them who through faith and patience* **inherit the promises** (Heb. 6:12)

Examine yourself, judge every known and doubtful sin, confess to Him, and be clean, and you need never fear the judgment, against which we are so earnestly warned."[11] (emphasis added)

The wise and faithful believer will take these warnings and encouragement to heart and ***press on toward the mark for the prize*** *[crown] of the high calling of God in Christ Jesus* (Phl 3:14).

A *glorious* crown awaits all the faithful (Jam 1:12)!

---

11) M.R. DeHaan, ***Studies in Hebrews*** (Kregel Publications, Grand Rapids, MI, 49501): 108

Warning # 4

Don't Cast Away Your Confidence

The fourth warning to believers, which is found in chapter 10 in the Book of Hebrews, provides a warning similar to the previous one in chapter 6; however, with possibly more severe consequences.

Hold Fast Your Confidence
Before presenting the warning, Paul reminds us to always encourage our fellow pilgrims in this world:

> *"23) Let us hold fast the confession of our hope without wavering, for He who promised is faithful. 24) And let us consider one another in order to stir up love and good works, 25) not forsaking the assembling of ourselves together, as is the manner of some, but exhorting one another, and so much the more as you see the Day approaching* (Hbr 10:23-25 – NKJV).

When COVID struck in 2020, it became impossible to gather with fellow believers. Since then, many have not returned to the church, making it difficult to fulfill the above exhortation. This is a critical reminder to find a good church home.

Believers need each other to help one another grow in their faith, particularly as we see the Day of the Lord's return fast approaching. We need to encourage one another to do the *good works* He has called us to do. We need each other to help pray for one another as the times and trials become worse. This fourth warning requires our faithfulness to achieve the promised reward.

Chapters 7, 8, and 9 in Hebrews provide a thorough and comprehensive description of Jesus Christ, who is our High Priest interceding for us in heaven. Jesus is here to help whenever we need Him; all we have to do is ask (Hbr 4:14-16).

Punishment for Willful Sinning

> *26) For if we sin willfully after we have received the knowledge of the truth, there no longer remains a sacrifice for sins, 27) but a certain fearful expectation of judgment, and fiery indignation which will devour the adversaries. 31) It is a fearful thing to fall into the hands of the living God.* (Hbr 10:26, 27, 31 – NKJV)

Notice that the Apostle Paul includes even himself (if we) in this stern warning against apostasy. A willful sin, in the eyes of God, is committed after receiving the full knowledge of the truth. This describes mature believers in Christ.

WARNING # 4 *Don't Castaway Your Confidence*

In Paul's day, this would have referred to Hebrew believers who had come to know Christ as their personal saviour and then decided to abandon the assembly of the church to return to Judaism.

For today's believers, the application is similar, where a willful sin is a deliberate and determined act of disobedience with full knowledge that it is wrong. This is different from normal sins out of weakness or ignorance, which He forgives:

If we confess our sins, He is faithful and just to forgive us our sins, and to cleanse us from all unrighteousness (1Jo 1:9 – NKJV).

The throne of Grace is available for all believers to take their sins to become fully restored.

However, because of willful sinning, the believer will one day face the Judgment Seat of Christ, where:

*10)...every one may receive the things done in his body, according to that he hath done, whether it be good or bad. 11) Knowing therefore **the terror of the Lord, we persuade men**;* (2Cr 5:10-11 – KJV).

When these believers appear before Christ, they will experience the awful ***terror of the Lord***.

Outer Darkness
In the Olivet Discourse, Jesus gave us a preview of what will happen to these unfaithful believers:

> *And cast ye the unprofitable servant into **outer darkness**: there shall be weeping and gnashing of teeth* (Mat 25:30 – KJV).

Knowing this, Apostle Paul included the following admonition in the fourth warning to the Hebrews:

> *31) It is a fearful thing to fall into the hands of the living God* (Hbr 10:26-31 – NKJV).

Inheritance in Jeopardy
Many in the church today may not be aware of the possible dangers that exist regarding our future inheritance.

> *23) And whatever you do, do it heartily, as to the Lord and not to men, 24) knowing that from the Lord you will receive the **reward of the inheritance**; for you serve the Lord Christ. 25) But **he who does wrong** will be repaid for what he has done, and **there is no partiality*** (Col 3:23-25).

The reward of the inheritance, which the Apostle Paul is describing in the above passage, is dependent on faithfulness. The just recompense of reward is based upon our trustworthy performance.

WARNING # 4 *Don't Castaway Your Confidence*

The Apostle Paul gives us many examples, which should have a sobering effect upon those Christians who are not truly being led by the Spirit of God, and are in danger of losing their inheritance in the Kingdom:

> *So I say, live by the Spirit, and you will not gratify the desires of the sinful nature...The acts of the sinful nature are obvious: sexual immorality, impurity and debauchery; idolatry and witchcraft; hatred, discord, jealousy, fits of rage, selfish ambition, dissensions, factions and envy; drunkenness, orgies, and the like. I warn you, as I did before, that those who live like this **will not inherit the kingdom of God**.*
> (Gal 5:16, 19-21 – NIV)

> *But among you there must not be even a hint of sexual immorality, or of any kind of impurity, or of greed, because these are improper for God's holy people. Nor should there be obscenity, foolish talk, or coarse joking, which are out of place, but rather thanksgiving. For of this you can be sure: No immoral, impure or greedy person – such a man is an idolater – **has any inheritance in the kingdom of Christ and of God**. Let no one deceive you with empty words, for because of such things God's wrath comes on those who are disobedient.* (Eph 5:3-6 – NIV)

Since then, you have been raised with Christ, set your hearts on things above, where Christ is seated at the right hand of God. Set your minds on things above, not on earthly things. For you died, and your life is now hidden with Christ in God. When Christ, who is your life, appears, then you also will appear with him in glory. Put to death, therefore, whatever belongs to your earthly nature: sexual immorality, impurity, lust, evil desires, and greed, which is idolatry. ***Because of these, the wrath of God is coming.*** *You used to walk in these ways, in the life you once lived. But now you must rid yourselves of all such things as these: anger, rage, malice, slander, and filthy language from your lips. Do not lie to each other, since you have taken off your old self with its practices and have put on the new self, which is being renewed in knowledge in the image of its Creator.*
(Col 3:1-10 – NIV)

This fourth warning in the book of Hebrews is to persuade all believers to turn from any sin while there is still time. The Day of Christ's soon return is rapidly drawing near. "***Repent, for the Kingdom of Heaven is at hand***" (Mat 3:3).

For I reckon that the sufferings of this present time are not worthy to be compared with the glory which shall be revealed in us (Rom 8:18 – NKJV).

Don't Cast Away Your Confidence

> *32) But recall the former days in which, after you were illuminated, you endured a great struggle with sufferings: 33) partly while you were made a spectacle both by reproaches and tribulations, and partly while you became companions of those who were so treated; 34) for you had compassion on me in my chains, and joyfully accepted the plundering of your goods, **knowing** that **you have a better** and an **enduring possession for yourselves in heaven.***
> (Hbr 10:32-34 – NKJV)

The Apostle Paul is reminding these believers that they are not like those who are willfully sinning. No, these believers have endured many trials for their faith and have experienced much tribulation. They showed compassion for him, even accepting the unjust seizure of their possessions, knowing greater rewards await them in heaven.

> *35) Therefore, do not cast away your confidence, which has great reward. 36) For you have **need of endurance**, so that after you have done the will of God, **you will receive the promise**:*
> *39 But we are not of those who draw back to perdition, but of those who believe to the **saving of the soul.*** (Hbr 10:35, 36, 39 – NKJV)

As we see the Day of the Lord's return drawing very near, Paul's admonition is for faithful believers to press on and not to give up, because we will realize the reward of the inheritance (Col 3:24) very soon.

Don't be like those who will become castaways due to their failure to allow the Holy Spirit to help overcome sin in their lives, but *"work out your own salvation with fear and trembling."* (Phl 2:12)

By allowing Christ to live His life in us, we will be able to *"press toward the goal for the **prize** of the upward call of God in Christ Jesus."* (Phl 3:14)

As the first warning taught us not to neglect so **great salvation** (Hbr 2:3), which is *the salvation of the soul*, this fourth warning illustrates how very imperative this teaching really is.

However, when the Son of Man comes,
Will He find [persistence in]^b faith
On the earth? (Luk 18:8b – AMP)

Is Jesus predicting that very few will exhibit faith that is persevering when He returns?

b) Marvin Vincent, ***Word Studies***

Warning # 5

Don't Refuse to Listen to Him

Readers are encouraged to pause for a moment to read the eleventh chapter of Hebrews, which testifies to God's faithfulness in the past as demonstrated by the great heroes of the faith. The 12th chapter then begins by referring back to their great faith:

> *Therefore, since we are surrounded by so great a cloud of witnesses [who by faith have testified to the truth of God's absolute faithfulness], stripping off every unnecessary weight and the sin which so easily and cleverly entangles us,* **let us run with endurance** *and* **active persistence the race** *that is* **set before us***,* (Hbr 12:1 – AMP)

Inspired by this great cloud of witnesses who relied upon God's faithfulness, we are encouraged to remove any sin from our lives and to finish the race that He has for us.

While many viewed their sojourn on the earth as foreigners, strangers, or pilgrims, they were looking for a *heavenly city*, which has foundations, whose builder and maker is God (Hbr 11:10, 16).

We are then warned, once again, to remember the story of Esau, *"who for one morsel of food sold his birthright. 17) For you know that afterward, when he wanted to inherit the blessing, he was rejected, for he found no place for repentance, though he sought it diligently with tears* (Hbr 12:16-17).

Esau lived for the present, not thinking of the consequences. This is a reminder that we need to keep our eyes on Jesus (Hbr 12:2) and the *prize* set before us. The cares and pleasures of this life could cause us to forfeit the blessing God has for us.

Paul then contrasts how Israel came to Mount Sinai: *"20)(For they could not endure what was commanded:* "*And if so much as a beast touches the mountain, it shall be stoned...21) And so terrifying was the sight that Moses said,* "*I am exceedingly afraid and trembling"*) (Hbr 12:20-21). After sharing the terrifying story of Moses under the old covenant, where the law was given on Mount Sinai, Paul tells us about the glorious Heavenly Jerusalem on Mount Zion in Hebrews 12:

*22) But you have come to Mount Zion and to the city of the living God, the **heavenly** Jerusalem, to an innumerable company of angels, 23) to the general assembly and **church of the firstborn who are registered in heaven**, to God the Judge of all, to the spirits of just men made perfect;*

WARNING # 5 *Don't Refuse to Listen to Him*

City of Reward
Mount Zion represents the Holy City, the New Jerusalem (*cf.* Rev 21:2, 10, 23), which will be the dwelling place for all those faithful believers who have qualified for the prize (Phl 4:13).

The goal of the Christian faith is to realize the *salvation of our soul* when we stand before Jesus at His Judgment Seat. If we are found faithful, we will receive the reward of our inheritance (Col 3:23-25), granting us the privilege of ruling and reigning with Jesus in the Holy City. All faithful believers will be honoured to live there for all eternity.

G.H. Lang saw this city as a *reward* for the *faithful*:

> "The heavenly portion is for that limited portion of the saved known to Scripture as "the *church* of the *firstborn ones* who are enrolled *in heaven*" (Heb 12:23). (1) Their calling to this superior dignity is of grace. (2) Their pathway to it is marked by sharing the sufferings of Christ. (3) Their attaining thereto is the reward that grace will give for the sufferings which grace enabled them to bear unto the end. They might have avoided the sufferings, as in fact many, alas, do; in which case they would have fallen short of the grace and have forfeited the reward."[12]

---

12) G.H. Lang, ***The Revelation of Jesus Christ*** (Schoettle Publishing, Hayesville, NC, 28904): 381

Because of the possibility of losing this wonderful reward, the fifth warning in the book of Hebrews is given by Jesus:

> *24) and to **Jesus**, the Mediator of **a new covenant** [uniting God and man], and to the sprinkled blood, which speaks [of mercy], a **better** and **nobler** and more **gracious message** than the blood of Abel [which cried out for vengeance]. 25) See to it that you **do not refuse [to listen to] Him** who is speaking [to you now]. For if those [sons of Israel] did not escape when they refused [to listen to] him who warned them on earth [revealing God's will], how much less will we escape **if we turn our backs on Him** who **warns from heaven?*** (Hbr 12:24-25 – AMP)

Fellow believer, Jesus is speaking to us right now! Are you truly listening to Him? He is offering you the magnificent privilege to share in His coming Kingdom!

All but Caleb and Joshua failed to listen to Him when they were offered possession in the land of Canaan. They all turned their backs and died in the wilderness. Their example was provided to show how they refused to listen. God has given us these examples so we don't make the same mistake. If we fail to heed the warning, we are in danger of missing the opportunity to rule and reign with Him!

WARNING # 5 *Don't Refuse to Listen to Him*   47

Millennial Kingdom Prize

*24) Do you not know that in a race all the runners run [their very best to win], but **only one receives the prize?** Run [your race] in such a way that you may seize the prize and make it yours!*

*27) But [like a boxer] I strictly discipline my body and make it my slave, so that, after I have preached [the gospel] to others, **I myself will not somehow be disqualified** [as unfit for service].*

(1 Cor 9:24, 27 – AMP)

The Apostle Paul wrote this to the Corinthian church to show that even he could be disqualified from receiving the prize. If this great Apostle was concerned for himself, shouldn't we also be concerned for ourselves?

Now is the time to take an inventory of our spiritual condition. Tomorrow could be too late! This fifth and final warning is given to make sure we are really listening to Him.

The warnings given in the book of Hebrews point to the importance of perseverance to be rewarded with our inheritance in the coming Millennial Kingdom.

Will He Find Faith?

In Luke 18:8b, Jesus told the parable of the persistent widow, ending with the question:

> *However, when the Son of Man comes,*
> *Will He find [persistence in] faith on the earth?*

Thanks to Marvin Vincent's insight, our Lord's rhetorical question might be paraphrased:

> *However, when the Son of Man comes,*
> *Will He find believers persevering in their faith?*

When the Lord returns, He will be looking for believers who are persevering in their faith.

This is precisely why we must examine ourselves now. Jesus will decide whether to grant us entry into the Millennial Kingdom based upon our faithful perseverance as we race for the prize.

May this short review of the five warnings in the book of Hebrews stir your heart to: *run with endurance and **active persistence** the race that is set before us* (Hbr 12:1 – AMP).

May the Lord move upon your heart as you draw closer to Him. He desires to tell every believer reading this booklet:

> *Well done, good and faithful servant...*
> *Enter into the joy of your Lord.*
> (Matthew 25:21)

Epilogue

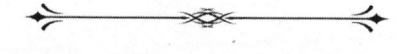

It is my heartfelt prayer that this booklet will help you realize the importance of the Great Salvation we have been given by our wonderful Lord and Saviour, Jesus Christ.

His great desire is to share His wonderful Kingdom with you. These five warnings in the book of Hebrews were given because He loves you.

In the closing passages of the Sermon on the Mount, Jesus told His **disciples**: *"13) Enter by the narrow gate; for wide is the gate and broad is the way that leads to destruction, and there are many who go in by it. 14) Because narrow is the gate and **difficult is the way which leads to life**, and there are few who **find it**"* (Mat 7:13-14 – NKJV).

May we all find it! And as the Apostle Peter said:

> The **approval of your faith**..may be discovered after scrutiny to result in praise and glory and honor at the time of the revelation of Jesus Christ; whom having not seen, you love because of His preciousness...you are to be rejoicing with an inexpressible and glorified joy upon the occasion of your receiving the promised **consummation of your faith** which is the **salvation of your souls**. (1Pe1:7-9)[13]

---

13) Kenneth Wuest, (W.B. Eerdmans Pub, *New Testament An Expanded Translation*, 1961): 549

Excerpt from THE COMING SPIRITUAL EARTHQUAKE by Cindy

An overcomer is a believer who has had an authentic experience with God. Though thrown into the furnace of affliction, they have come forth as pure gold. The overcomer is born through the victory they receive by trusting in Jesus Christ. Learning to be an overcomer is perhaps the most difficult thing to do on this earth as a human being. Possessing impressive credentials and degrees offer little solace when it comes to where the "rubber meets the road." Every professing Christian must learn to be an overcomer through faith and total trust in their Savior. In Matthew 11:28-30, Jesus urges: *"Come unto me, all ye that labour and are heavy laden, and I will give you rest. Take my yoke upon you, and learn of me; for I am meek and lowly in heart: and ye shall find rest unto your souls. For my yoke is easy, and my burden is light."* The overcomers take their agony and burdens to the mighty counselor. Through prayer and trust, Jesus leads the downcast believer to "green pasture." The sting of the adversary is somehow turned to sweet victory. Christ alone is able to provide the peace that passes all understanding. While every believer will have trials and testing in this world, Christ reminded us to be of good cheer because He overcame this world. As believers, we find our sweet victory in Him! Overcomers are believers who find their strength and help in Him--not through man, but by the power of the Son of God. A genuine overcomer follows in Christ's footsteps. They learn to "take it on the chin" and to "take it to the cross." Whatever the world dishes out is handled with prayer and placed on the altar before God. By offering everything to Christ, they find hope and sufficiency in Him. Being an overcomer is what being a Christian is all about. Through the trials of this life, the overcomers' faith is put on trial and thereby confirmed as Holy evidence before a mighty God, it is authentic. As our example, Jesus endured the cross for the joy set before Him. Overcomers have the victory because of His victory. Through His victory, the overcomer is able to walk in newness of life. The overcomer knows: they have been crucified with Christ and their old life is gone (Gal 2:20). By dying to self, the overcomer experiences the joy of Christ's triumph in their life. Finally, an overcomer is grateful and humble: for they know of God's rich mercy and marvelous grace. If it wasn't for Christ, they would be doomed. Out of this gratitude, rises the song of gladness and praise. An overcomers' heart bursts forth with praise and adoration unto their God for the victory He provides. The overcomer knows, first hand, that while weeping may endure for the night: joy cometh in the morning!

Bibliography

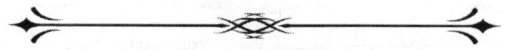

Chitwood, Arlen L.– *So Great Salvation*, The Lamp Broadcast, © 2020
(www.LampBroadcast.org)

Crawford, Scott – *Hebrews: Five Warnings for Believers*, Word of Truth Press, © 2006
(www.WordofTruthClass.org)

DeHaan, M.R. – *Studies In Hebrews*, Kregel Publications, © 1996

Govett, Robert – *Govett on Hebrews*, Schoettle Publishing, © 2010

Hollandsworth, James S. – *The End of the Pilgrimage*, Hollypublishing © 2015
(www.TruthOverTraditions.com)

Ironside, Harry A. – *Except Ye Repent*, Baker Books, © 1937

Lang, G.H. – *The Revelation of Jesus Christ*, Schoettle Publishing © 2006
(www.SchoettlePublishing.com)

Lever, Martha – *Rightly Dividing the Word of Truth*, Schoettle Publishing, © 2011

Mauro, Philip – *God's Pilgrims*, Schoettle Publishing, © 1984

Panton, D.M. – *The Judgment Seat of Christ*, Schoettle Publishing, © 1984

Wuest, Kenneth S. – *The New Testament An Expanded Translation*, W.B. Eerdmans Publishing Company, © 1961

ABBREVIATIONS

Books of the Bible

Old Testament (OT)

Genesis (Gen)
Exodus (Exd)
Leviticus (Lev)
Numbers (Num)
Deuteronomy (Deu)
Joshua (Jos)
Judges (Jdg)
Ruth (Rth)
1 Samuel (1Sa)
2 Samuel (2Sa)
1 Kings (1Ki)
2 Kings (2Ki)
1 Chronicles (1Ch)
2 Chronicles (2Ch)
Ezra (Ezr)
Nehemiah (Neh)
Esther (Est)
Job (Job)
Psalms (Psa)
Proverbs (Pro)
Ecclesiastes (Ecc)
Solomon (Sgs)
Isaiah (Isa)
Jeremiah (Jer)
Lamentations (Lam)
Ezekiel (Eze)
Daniel (Dan)
Hosea (Hsa)
Joel (Joe)
Amos (Amo)
Obadiah (Oba)
Jonah (Jon)
Micah (Mic)
Nahum (Nah)
Habakkuk (Hab)
Zephaniah (Zep)
Haggai (Hag)
Zechariah (Zec)
Malachi (Mal)

New Testament (NT)

Matthew (Mat)
Mark (Mar)
Luke (Luk)
John (Jhn)
Acts (Act)
Romans (Rom)
1 Corinthians (1Cr)
2 Corinthians (2Cr)
Galatians (Gal)
Ephesians (Eph)
Philippians (Phl)
Colossians (Col)
1 Thessalonians (1Th)
2 Thessalonians (2Th)
1 Timothy (1Ti)
2 Timothy (2Ti)
Titus (Tts)
Philemon (Phm)
Hebrews (Hbr)
James (Jam)
1 Peter (1Pe)
2 Peter (2Pe)
1 John (1Jo)
2 John (2Jo)
3 John (3Jo)
Jude (Jud)
Revelation (Rev)

Courtesy of Blue Letter Bible (www.BlueLetterBible.org)

Appendix – Signs of Christ's Coming

Many modern Bible teachers and students believe that the rebirth of the nation of Israel represents the budding of the ***fig tree*** that Jesus described to His disciples as He sat on the Mount of Olives, and we are living in the generation that won't pass away before He returns.

Verily I say unto you, this generation shall not pass, till all these things be fulfilled.
(Matthew 24:34 – KJV)

With Israel becoming a nation in 1948, we have been alerted that the Lord's return is fast approaching. Jesus also told his disciples a second sign to look for in the parable of Noah:

As it was in the days of Noah, so it will be at the coming of the Son of Man.
(Matthew 24:37 – NIV)

A careful study of Genesis 6 will alert the reader to the fact that living in these end times is almost parallel to the time before the flood. The world has become a great cesspool of corruption, violence, sex, drugs, idolatry, witchcraft, and other perversions. Reading the account in Genesis is like reading today's newspaper or listening to the daily news. In the Lord's parable concerning Noah, Jesus was also giving us a second important sign that His return is drawing very near. Several years ago, a famous comet passed through our solar system, and it was hailed as the most-watched comet of all time.

April 8, 1997

Comet Hale-Bopp Over New York City
Credit and Copyright: J. Sivo
http://antwrp.gsfc.nasa.gov/apod/ap970408.html

"What's that point of light above the World Trade Center? It's Comet Hale-Bopp! Both faster than a speeding bullet and able to "leap" tall buildings in its single orbit, Comet Hale-Bopp is also bright enough to be seen even over the glowing lights of one of the world's premier cities. In the foreground lies the East River, while much of New York City's Lower Manhattan can be seen between the river and the comet."

As it was in the days of Noah,
so it will be at the coming of the Son of Man.
(Matthew 24:37 – NIV)

These words from our wonderful Lord have several applications about the Tribulation period that is about to ensnare this world.

APPENDIX – *Signs of Christ's Coming*

Seas Lifted Up

Throughout the Old Testament, the time of the coming Tribulation period is described as the time when the "seas have lifted up," and also as coming in as a "flood" (please see Jeremiah 51:42, Hosea 5:10, Daniel 11:40, and Psalm 93:3-4 for just a few examples).

This is a direct parallel to the time of Noah, when the Great Flood of water came to wipe out every living creature except for righteous Noah and his family, and the pairs of animals God spared. While God said He would never flood the earth again with water, the coming Judgment will be by fire (II Peter 3:10). The book of Revelation shows that approximately three billion people will perish in the terrible time that lies ahead (see Revelation 6:8 and 9:15).

2 Witnesses

A guiding principle of God is to establish a matter based upon the witness of two or more:

> *...a matter must be established by the testimony of two or three witnesses* (Deu 19:15 – NIV)

In 1994, God was able to get the attention of mankind when Comet Shoemaker-Levy crashed into Jupiter on the 9th of Av (on the Jewish calendar). Interestingly, this Comet was named after the "two" witnesses who first discovered it.

In 1995, "two" more astronomers also discovered another comet. It was called Comet Hale-Bopp, and it reached its closest approach to planet Earth on March 23, 1997. It has been labeled as the most widely viewed comet in the history of mankind.

Scientists have determined that Comet Hale-Bopp's orbit brought it to our solar system 4,465 years ago (see Notes 1 and 2 below). In other words, the comet made its appearance near Earth in 1997 and also in 2468 BC. Remarkably, this comet preceded the Great Flood by 120 years! God warned Noah of this in Genesis 6:3:

> *My Spirit shall not strive with man forever, for he is indeed flesh; yet his days shall be one hundred and twenty years.*

Days of Noah

What does all of this have to do with the Lord's return? Noah was born around 2948 BC, and Genesis 7:11 tells us that the Flood took place when Noah was 600, or in 2348 BC.

Remember, our Lord told us: ***"As it was in the days of Noah, so it will be at the coming of the Son of Man.*** (Matthew 24:37 – NIV) In the original Greek, it says: ***"exactly like"*** it was, so it will be when He comes (see Strong's #5618).

During the days of Noah, Comet Hale-Bopp arrived on the scene as a harbinger of the Great Flood. Just as this same comet appeared before the Flood, could its arrival again in 1997 be a sign that God's final Judgment, also known as the time of Jacob's Trouble, is about to begin?

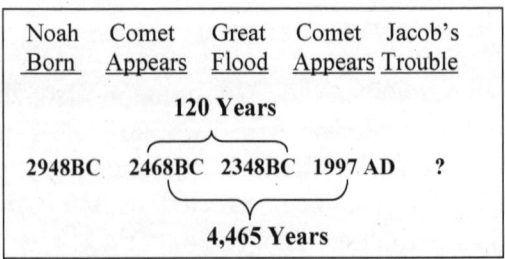

APPENDIX – *Signs of Christ's Coming*

Comet Hale-Bopp arrived 120 years before the Flood as a warning to mankind. Only righteous Noah heeded God's warning and built the ark, as God instructed. By faith, Noah was obedient to God and, as a result, saved himself and his family from destruction.

Remember, Jesus told us His return would be preceded by great heavenly signs: *"And there shall be signs in the sun, and in the moon, and in the stars; and upon the earth distress of nations, with perplexity; the sea and the waves roaring..."* (Luke 21:25)

> **Jesus was asked 3 questions by the disciples:**
> *"Tell us, (1) when shall these things be"* (the *destruction of the city of Jerusalem), (2) what shall be the **sign** of thy coming, and (3) of the end of the world?"* (Matthew 24:3)

Just as this large comet appeared as a 120-year warning to Noah, its arrival in 1997 tells us that Jesus is getting ready to return again. Is this the **"Sign"** Jesus referred to?

Sign of Christ's Coming

The **first** question had to do with events that were fulfilled in 70 AD. The **third** question has to do with the future time at the very end of the age.

The **second** question, however, has to do with the time of Christ's second coming. Jesus answered this second question in His description of the days of Noah found in Matthew 24:33-39:

> ³⁷ **But as the days of Noe were, so shall also the coming of the Son of man be.** ⁽³⁸⁾*For as in the days that were before the flood they were eating and drinking, marrying and giving in marriage, until the day that Noe entered into the ark,* ⁽³⁹⁾ *And knew not until the flood came, and took them all away; so shall also the coming of the Son of man be.*

Jesus is telling us that the **_sign_** of His coming will be as it was during the days of Noah. As Comet Hale-Bopp was a sign to the people in Noah's day, its arrival in 1997 is a sign that Jesus is coming back again soon. Comet Hale-Bopp could be the very sign Jesus was referring to, which would announce His return for His faithful.

Remember, Jesus said, *"**exactly as** it was in the days of Noah, so will it be when He returns."* The appearance of Comet Hale-Bopp in 1997 is a strong indication that the Tribulation period is about to begin, but before then, Jesus is coming for His bride!

Keep looking up! Jesus is coming very soon!

As Noah prepared for the destruction God warned him about 120 years before the Flood, Jesus has given mankind a final warning that the Tribulation period is about to begin. The horrible destruction on 9/11 is only a precursor of what is about to take place on planet Earth. We need to be wise like Noah and prepare. Always remember our Lord's important instructions in Luke 21:36:

APPENDIX – *Signs of Christ's Coming*

(36) Watch ye therefore, and <u>pray always</u>, that ye may be <u>accounted worthy to escape</u> all these things that shall come to pass, and to stand before the Son of man (Luke 21:36).

Footnotes to Appendix 1

(1) The original orbit of Comet Hale-Bopp was calculated to be approximately 265 years by engineer George Sanctuary in his article, *Three Craters In Israel*, published on 3/31/01 found in the Supplemental Articles for *Coming Spiritual Earthquake*.

Comet Hale-Bopp's orbit around the time of the Flood changed from 265 years to about 4,200 years. Because the plane of the comet's orbit is perpendicular to the earth's orbital plane (ecliptic), Mr. Sanctuary noted: "A negative time increment was used for this simulation...to back the comet away from the earth.... past Jupiter... and then out of the solar system. The simulation suggests that the past-past orbit had a very eccentric orbit with a period of only 265 years. When the comet passed Jupiter (*around 2203BC*) its orbit was deflected upward, coming down near the earth 15 months later with the comet's period changed from 265 years to about (*4,200*) years."

(2) Don Yeomans, with NASA's Jet Propulsion Laboratory, made the following observations regarding the comet's orbit: "By integrating the above orbit forward and backward in time until the comet leaves the planetary system and then referring the osculating orbital elements...the following orbital periods result: Original orbital period before entering planetary system

= 4200 years. Future orbital period after exiting the planetary system = 2380 years."

This analysis can be found at:

http://www2.jpl.nasa.gov/comet/ephemjpl6.html

Based upon the above two calculations we have the following:

265 [a] + 4,200 [b] = 4,465 Years

1997 AD − 4,465 Years = 2468 BC = Hale Bopp arrived

(a) Orbit period calculated by George Sanctuary before deflection around 2203 BC.

(b) Orbit period calculated by Don Yeomans after 1997 visit.

THE BRIDE (Matthew 25:1-13) by Cindy
A lamp with oil
All 10 did possess
But, remember, 5 were wise
And 5 were foolish.
Those who were wise
Heeded the call
By hearing God's voice:
"Give me your all"
The foolish however
Squandered their worth
They did not shine for Jesus
Nor the people on earth.
They heard "The Cry"
Along with the wise
This is how the foolish
Were taken by surprise:
Their light became impoverished
For their joy did not spread
The 'oil of gladness' for them
Flickered out instead.
But the wise grew brighter
With a special over-flow
The more they loved Jesus
They gained a purer glow.
Though the cry was mighty
Five questioned the call
They could not comprehend:
'Come give me your all.'
For if they truly loved Him
They would have understood the plea
For hidden in the message is:
'My Beloved come to Me.'
The 5 wise virgins heard this impassioned cry
….And answered 'Yes, my Beloved,
I am coming, it is I'
So they laid it all down
Living only to serve
The moral of the 10 virgins is:
Each got what they deserve.

Special Invitation

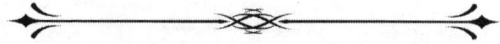

This booklet was primarily written for those who have been born again. If you have never been born again, would you like to be? The Bible shows that it's simple to be saved...

- **Realize you are a sinner.**
  "As it is written, There is none righteous, no, not one:" (Romans 3:10)
  "... for there is no difference. For all have sinned, and come short of the glory of God;" (Romans 3:22-23)
- **Realize you CAN NOT save yourself.**
  "But we are all as an unclean thing, and all our righteousness are as filthy rags; ..." (Isaiah 64:6)
  "Not by works of righteousness which we have done, but according to his mercy he saved us..." (Titus 3:5)
- **Realize that Jesus Christ died on the cross to pay for your sins.**
  "Who his own self bare our sins in his own body on the tree,..." (I Peter 2:24)
  "... Unto him that loved us, and washed us from our sins in his own blood," (Revelation 1:5)
- **Simply by faith receive Jesus Christ.**
  "But as many as received him, to them gave he power to become the sons of God, even to them that believe on his name:" (John 1:12)
  "...Sirs, what must I do to be saved? And they said, Believe on the Lord Jesus Christ, and thou shalt be saved, and thy house." (Acts 16:30-31)

WOULD YOU LIKE TO BE SAVED?

If you would like to be saved, believe on the Lord Jesus Christ right now by making this acknowledgment in your heart:

> Lord Jesus, I know that I am a sinner, and unless You save me, I am lost forever. I thank You for dying for me at Calvary. By faith, I come to You now, Lord, the best way I know how, and ask You to save me. I believe that God raised You from the dead and acknowledge You as my personal Saviour.

If you believed on the Lord, this is the most important moment of your life. You are now saved by the precious blood of Jesus Christ, which was shed for you and your sins. Now that you have believed on Jesus as your personal Saviour, you will want to find a Church where you can be baptized as your first act of obedience, and where the Word of God is taught so you can continue to grow in your faith. Ask the Holy Spirit to help you as you read the Bible to learn all that God has for your life.

Also, please see the Bibliography, as well as the pages that follow, for information on several books that will help you on your wonderful journey and help you prepare for the days ahead.

About The Author

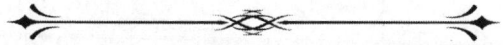

Jim Harman has been a Christian for more than 48 years. He has diligently studied the Word of God with a particular emphasis on Prophecy. Jim has written several books, and the most essential titles are available at www.ProphecyCountdown.com: ***The Coming Spiritual Earthquake, The Kingdom, Overcomers' Guide To The Kingdom, Calling All Overcomers, Come Away My Beloved, Daniel's Prophecies Unsealed, and Salvation of the Soul,*** which have been widely distributed around the world. These books will encourage you to continue *"Looking"* for the Lord's soon return.

Jim's professional experience included being a Certified Public Accountant (CPA) and a Certified Property Manager (CPM). He had an extensive background in both public accounting and financial management with several well-known national firms.

Jim was fortunate to have been acquainted with several mature believers who understand and teach the deeper truths of the Bible. It is Jim's strong desire that many will come to realize the vital importance of seeking the Kingdom and seeking Christ's righteousness as we approach the soon return of our Lord and Saviour Jesus Christ.

The burden of Jim's heart is to see many believers come to know the joy of Christ's triumph in their lives as they become true overcomers, qualified and ready to rule and reign with Christ in the coming Kingdom.

To contact Jim for questions, to arrange for speaking engagements, or to order multiple copies of his books:

Jim Harman
P.O. Box 941612
Maitland, FL
JimHarmanCPA@gmail.com

Endtimes

The Bible indicates that we are living in the final days and Jesus Christ is getting ready to return very soon. This book was written to help Christians prepare for what lies ahead. The Word of God indicates that the Tribulation Period is rapidly approaching and that the Antichrist is getting ready to emerge on the world scene.

Jesus promised His disciples that there is a way to escape the horrible time of testing and persecution that will soon devastate this planet. The main purpose of this book is to help you get prepared so you will rule and reign with Jesus when He returns.

HOW STANDING BEFORE CHRIST CAN BE OUR MOST GLORIOUS MOMENT

When Jesus returns, He will review all of our lives to determine whether we have been faithful and obedient doers of His Word. The purpose of this book is to prepare believers so they will be able to hear Him say:
"Well done, good and faithful servant....
Enter into the joy of your lord" (Matthew 25:21).

MUST-READ FOR ALL BELIEVERS

NEW DISCOVERY – LEARN ABOUT
- The salvation of our spirit and soul.
- What Jesus meant by *"take up your cross."*
- How the Word of God can save our souls.
- When the salvation of our soul takes place.
- Sign of Christ's Coming

FREE copy: www.ProphecyCountdown.com

Order your copy today ***Paperback – eBook – Audio*** Editions

The Final Countdown is a sequel to the Top-10 Best-Selling ***Daniel's Prophecies Unsealed***. Thanks to the incredible discovery by Dr. Christian Widener, the book of Daniel has been unsealed. James Harman has summarized this important message to help prepare the end-time Church for the days ahead. Daniel was told that the words would be closed up and sealed until the time of the end. Dr. Widener's finding is truly a treasured gem you don't want to miss.

Now is the time to prepare and help others prepare before the time of the Great Tribulation arrives. Jesus provides a way of escape for those blameless believers who are ready. The purpose of this book is to help you prepare.

FREE copy: www.ProphecyCountdown.com

Order your copy today ***Paperback*** – ***eBook*** – ***Audio*** Editions

The Open Door was written to reveal the Scriptures that will help you learn how to watch for Christ's return. The message in this timely prophetic book will help you understand:

- The Judgment Seat Christ will not be an award ceremony for every Christian.
- How you can obtain the 5 Crowns mentioned in the Bible.
- How you can ensure you will be part of the Bride of Christ.
- How you can reign and rule with the King of the Universe.

Jesus went away almost 2,000 years ago, and He is in the process of preparing a Holy City for all overcoming believers. Lyn Mize has given us an excellent resource that can be instrumental in helping us get ready.

Available From Amazon.com

Paperback**, **Kindle**,* **and** ***Audible **Editions**

"Go your way Daniel, because the words are closed up and sealed until the time of the end...none of the wicked will understand, but those who are wise will understand."
(Daniel 12:9-10)

When Jesus came the first time, the wise men of the day were aware of His soon arrival and they were actively looking for Him. Today, those who are wise will be passionately helping others by turning them to righteousness. Those doing so will *"shine like the stars forever and ever."*

May the Lord grant us a heart of wisdom to understand the time we are living in so we can prepare for what lies ahead!
FREE copy: www.ProphecyCountdown.com

Order your copy today *Paperback – eBook – Audio* Editions

Come Away My Beloved is a refreshing commentary. You will realize why this ancient love story has perplexed Bible students and commentators down through the ages.

Written almost 3,000 years ago, this brilliant Song of Love reflects God's desire for every man and woman.

This book will revive your heart with a fervent love for your Saviour. It will also help you prepare for your glorious wedding day when Jesus returns for His devoted bride.

Allow this beautiful story of love and passion to ignite a flame in your heart and let this inspirational Song arouse your heart to join in the impassioned cry with the rest of the bride: *"Make haste, my beloved…come quickly…"*
FREE copy: www.ProphecyCountdown.com

Order your copy today: ***Paperback – eBook*** Editions

Perplexed by the book of Revelation? Not sure what all the signs, symbols, and metaphors really mean? Jim Harman's latest work unravels Apostle John's remarkable revelation of Jesus Christ and what's in store for the inhabitants of planet Earth.

One of the central messages in the book of Revelation is that God is calling men to be genuine overcomers. Jesus Christ has been sent out from the throne of God to conquer men's hearts so they can also be overcomers.

The reader will come away with a new and enlightened understanding of what the last book in God's Word is all about. Understand the book of Revelation and why it is so important for believers living in the last days of the Church age.

FREE copy: www.ProphecyCountdown.com

Order your copy today: ***Paperback – eBook*** Editions

Once a person is saved, the number one priority should be seeking entrance into the Kingdom through the salvation of their soul. It is pictured as a runner in a race seeking a prize represented by a crown that will last forever.

The "Traditional" teaching on the "THE KINGDOM" has taken the Church captive into believing all Christians will rule and reign with Christ, no matter if they have lived faithful and obedient lives, or if they have been slothful and disobedient. Find out the important Truth before Jesus Christ returns.

Jesus Christ is returning for His faithful overcoming followers. Don't miss the opportunity of ruling and reigning with Christ in the coming KINGDOM!

FREE copy: www.ProphecyCountdown.com

Order your copy today: ***Paperback – eBook*** Editions

Get ready to climb back up the Mountain to listen to Christ's teachings once again. Though you may have read His great *Sermon on the Mount* many times, discover exciting promises that many have missed.

The purpose of this book is to help Christians be the Overcomers Jesus wants them to be and to help them gain their own entrance in the coming Kingdom. Also, learn about:
- Beatitudes Link with the Fruit of the Spirit
- What the "law of Christ" really is
- The critical importance of the "Lord's prayer"
- How to be an Overcomer
- New song entitled: LOOKING FOR THE SON

FREE copy: www.ProphecyCountdown.com

Order your copy today *Paperback – eBook – Audio* Editions

LOOKING FOR THE SON
Lyrics by Jim Harman
Listen to this Song on the Home Page of
Prophecy Countdown

Lyric
There's a fire burning in my heart
Yearning for the Lord to come,
  and His Kingdom come to start
Soon He'll come.....so enter the narrow gate
Even though you mock me now...
  He'll come to set things straight
Watch how I'll leave in the twinkling of an eye
Don't be surprised when I go up in the sky
There's a fire burning in my heart
Yearning for my precious Lord
And His Kingdom come to start
Your love of this world, has forsaken His
It leaves me knowing that you could have had it all
Your love of this world, was oh so reckless
I can't help thinking
You would have had it all
Looking for the Son
(Tears are gonna fall, not looking for the Son
You had His holy Word in your hand
(You're gonna wish you had listened to me)
And you missed it...for your self
(Tears are gonna fall, not looking for the Son)
Brother, I have a story to be told
It's the only one that's true
And it should've made your heart turn
Remember me when I rise up in the air
Leaving your home down here
For true Treasures beyond compare

Your love of this world, has forsaken His
It leaves me knowing that you could have had it all
Your love of this world, was oh so reckless
I can't help thinking
You would have had it all
(Lyrics in parentheses represent background vocals)
Looking for the Son
(Tears are gonna fall, not looking for the Son)
You had His holy Word in your hand
(You're gonna wish you had listened to me)
And you lost it...for your self
(Tears are gonna fall, not looking for the Son)
You would have had it all
Looking for the Son
You had His holy Word in your hand
But you missed it... for your self
Lov'n the world....not the open door
Down the broad way... blind to what life's really for
Turn around now...while there still is time
Learn your lesson now or you'll reap just what you sow
(You're gonna wish you had listened to me)
You would have had it all
(Tears are gonna fall, not looking for the Son)
You would have had it all
(You're gonna wish you had listened to me)
It all, it all, it all
(Tears are gonna fall, not looking for the Son)
You would have had it all
(You're gonna wish you had listened to me)
Looking for the Son
(Tears are gonna fall, not looking for the Son)
You had His holy Word in your hand
(You're gonna wish you had listened to me)

LOOKING FOR THE SON

And you missed it…for yourself
(Tears are gonna fall, not looking for the Son)
You would have had it all
(You're gonna wish you had listened to me)
Looking for the Son
(Tears are gonna fall, not looking for the Son)
You had His holy Word in your hand
(You're gonna wish you had listened to me)
But you missed it
You missed it
You missed it
You missed it.…for yourself

Scripture Summary
Jeremiah 25:4-8
Habakkuk 2:2
Matthew 6:20
Matthew 6:33
Matthew 7:13
Matthew 22:11-14
Matthew 25:10-13
Luke 21:34-36
Luke 24:332
John 3:16-17
I Corinthians 15:52

Scripture Summary
Galatians 6:7
Philippians 1:3-6
II Timothy 3:16
Titus 2:13
II Peter 3:9
II Peter 3:4
I John 1:9
I John 2:15
Revelation 3:10
Revelation 3:14-22
Revelation 4:1
Revelation 20:4-6
Revelation 21:7
Revelation 22:17

(For more information, please see:
www.ProphecyCountdown.com)
© Copyright 2011-26,
Prophecy Countdown Publications, LLC

The Day of the Lord is Near!

The Coming Spiritual Earthquake

by James T. Harman

"The Message presented in this book is greatly needed to awaken believers to the false ideas many have when it comes to the Rapture. I might have titled it: THE RAPTURE EARTHQUAKE!"
Ray Brubaker - God's News Behind the News

"If I am wrong, anyone who follows the directions given in this book will be better off spiritually. If I am right, they will be among the few to escape the greatest spiritual calamity of the ages."
Jim Harman - Author

**MUST READING FOR EVERY CHRISTIAN!
HURRY! BEFORE IT IS TOO LATE!**